VARIOUS ORBITS

Books by Thom Ward

Small Boat with Oars of Different Size
Tumblekid
Various Orbits

VARIOUS ORBITS

Poems by
Thom Ward

Carnegie Mellon University Press
Pittsburgh 2004

Acknowledgments

Grateful acknowledgment is made to the editors of these journals, newspapers and on-line magazines where many of the poems, or earlier versions of them, have appeared: *The American Literary Review*: "Inquiries and Meanderings: Almost a Love Poem" and "We Cannot Buy Cliffs Notes"; *Artful Dodge*: "At the Department of Motor Vehicles"; *Barkeater*: "According to the Crippled Angel"; *TheBlueMoon.com*: "After Decades of Silence, Toilet Speaks" and "Poof"; *The Bookpress*: "Cities Built Around Branches Built Around Flesh," "Harvest Festival, Tahaughnik, New York" and "Viagra Falls"; *Chelsea*: "Though Monarchs Exploit the Disparity Among Us"; *The Cider Press Review*: "When We Lie Down Beneath Vanilla Wood"; *The Clackamas Literary Review*: "Enough" and "Harvest Festival, Tahaughnik, New York"; *The Comstock Review*: "Saranac"; *The Denver Quarterly*: "Seneca"; *Desperate Act*: "Vitamins or Nautilus" and "Viagra Falls"; *Earth's Daughters*: "August Evening, Bright Hill Farm"; *The Journal*: "Having Evolved from Grass"; *Kestrel*: "The Bible on the Counter in Pat Verrazano's Paint Shop," "Having Evolved from Stones" and "Moonfabulousmoonfib"; *Margie*: "Beets" and "Cycling Through Taylor's Basin"; *The Marlboro Review*: "What Happens Without Fanfare" and "Wreckage"; *The Nation*: "Wherever the Wander Leads"; *The North American Review*: "Joseph and the Boss"; *nycBigCityLit.com*: "Cross-Country, Gershwin, Pizza"; *Quarterly West*: "American Fragment" and "Cross-Country, Gershwin, Pizza"; *Rattapallax*: "A Brief Epistle to Those Who Worked These Fields and Are Now Long Dead" and "For Barbie, Who, After Much Vodka, to Celebrate Her Birthday, Spent the Night with Her Sister"; *Rattle*: "Now That You've Anchored"; *River Oak Review*: "Such Family, Such Yule"; *Salamander*: "Ontario"; *The Sporting News*: "Cheesehead"; *Tar River Poetry*: "Do Something Useful" and "Night Game"; *The Texas Observer*: "Cycling Through Taylor's Basin" and "Enough"; *Two Rivers Review*: "Third Night in San Francisco" and "When the Mother of the Bride Is Dying." "American Fragment" also appeared in the book *Voices in the Gallery: Writers on Art* (The University of Rochester Press). Thanks to the Constance Saltonstall Foundation for the Arts for a creative writing fellowship that enabled me to complete many of the poems in this book. Thanks also to Jerry Costanzo and Cynthia Lamb of Carnegie Mellon University Press.

The Publication of this book is supported by a grant from the Pennsylvania Council on the Arts.

PENNSYLVANIA
COUNCIL
ON THE
ARTS

Contents

III

for Barbara
terra firma

and for Kasey, Peter and Taryn
our satellites

"Heart, moon, bone . . . bone, moon, heart.
Do I dare row across
The moat of the Milky Way?
What has night ever meant but night?"

—the lines Prufrock forgot to say

I

Wreckage

Zipped pink behind bars
this baby says
ha!
and means it.
The room crackles,
uncurls a fist.
Though the secret
of being perfectly dull
is to answer
every question, just once
I'd like to say
ha!
and mean it. As in
harmonium or *havoc*.
If I told you
illegal immigrants
live beneath my father's
bed, reach up at night
and drop polished stones
on his pillow,
would you think of mercy
or justice? Somewhere else
a woman acquires
leashes strong enough
for the wild dogs of irony,
even as her lover
trudges around a lake,
passes a friend
going the opposite way, quips,
Men jog together

whether they jog together
or apart. I believe
our fictions more forgiving
than the truths
behind them, it's possible
to confuse snowflakes
with success, that luck
is a pocket of old mistakes
turned inside out.
All this I believe,
at least until Thursday.
You can't
depend on your eyes
when your imagination
is muzzled, the famous author
told the audience
she'd relinquished drinking
but everyone
could smell the poetry
on her breath.
Just once
I'd like to say
ha!
and mean it, understand
without understanding.
If expectation plus
reality equals disillusionment,
who among us
will cross the border
into the country
of my father's sleep?
ha!   ba!
I believe I am cold,

have lost the ashes
on my face,
this child's elocution,
and the felicity
of your silence
which I promise
to keep close
as if it were
anything but itself—
a blotch of mud
or crumpled leaf,
a polished stone
lodged in the pocket
of the shirt I wear
as I walk through
my impoverished
attempts to speak,
the sharp light
of each hour's doubt
and frustration,
this clickity-clack
blue-veined volt world
we love but cannot trust,
all of us, scattering
wreckage in our wake,
in search of something
like justice, something
like mercy.

Beets

Sliced thick and moist and spongy,
so many purple ventricles
pulsing on my plate.
Beets. From the garden or the can,

anchored by a stubborn
vegetable suction, these little hearts
pump juice, bloody-sticky juice
seeking the warm source of itself.

How many times did I lift
fork loads of spuds and brace
for a good belt of beet?
They stain all attempts

at memory, for what else
is the past but a swollen root.
Summer evenings and burgers,
we sit across the kitchen table,

the hills and glens of the famous
food groups. My brother and I
apportioned six beets each, each
of them eager to spoil our corn.

What else? Well, it's hot.
Outside kids are yelling,
some are kicking the can.
Our sitter on the phone

with her gaggle of pals
is no easy bird. We've got to eat.
And these beets how they bleed
inexhaustible flows. For whatever

reason my brother embarks
on a furious voyage, lets his quota slosh
over the deck of his tongue.
He's spooning juice and humming.

This is too much.
So I scoop and spoon-load
and let fly a purple bullet
that thumps against his face

with a fantail spray. He screams,
You jerk! and flies from the table
toward the sitter and my future
a bad consequence. Which gets

me thinking—what is it
with beets? Perhaps
they remind me of those things
in myself intolerable

to myself, how the world presents
a menu of distasteful
situations of which
we have no recourse

but to swallow, choke down.
Then again I might hate beets
just because I hate beets,
each of our appetites

possessing its own limit.
Who knows. And I suspect
it's somewhat unhealthy
to overthink why we struggle

with our vegetables and fruits.
Still, I'm curious
if my brother finished off
those stubborn hearts

he was apportioned. Peeling
back the edge of the place mat,
deliberate and slow,
(if I scare them they might squeal)

I find beets blue and withered,
huddled like the bums who wait
for the last bus. They've lost a lot
of blood. Someone should put them

out of their misery, the dust pan,
the disposal so close. But I can't
do anything except whisper—
It's OK . . . We're going now . . . Take care

Night Game

Fat, blistered and weary,
the moon is the best
clutch hitter we've got.
Everyone wants
his autograph, a piece
of his jersey. He just wants
a shower and a good steak.
Pitchers rarely fool him
with their off-speed stuff.
After a called third strike
he never mopes
or blames it on the stars.

According to the Crippled Angel

living in our gutters the elementary backstroke
is civilization's greatest achievement, enables

anyone to float through Aristophanes' ink.
What separates the tragic from the comic
is how the latter drops the curtain just before

it gets ugly. Why not bring licorice to the annuals,
even those with bad attitudes, why not plant

questions to address the anxiety that works
like complex math, but without the dust
from chalk. Can the birth of a tenet overcome

the death of a clown? Should we puncture hot dogs
with these forks or scuttle after Christ? What if

similes are just old smiles refusing their collapse:
almost-day, maybe-day, seldom-day saints.
The truth is money doesn't care about us, the thoughts

we lend to brussels sprouts, though it's possible
to hide under malaprops when trouble comes looking.

In any case, the morning snow has decided to gloss
the gutters and the roof, the wings now folded
among leaf mold and mud, the shriveled leg

which aches to be symbolic of the mortal heart's
disfigurements, guardedly balanced between foolishness

and pride. For what option do we own but to welcome
our share of weeping, all the rogue misdemeanors
and felonies against love.

Cities Built Around Branches Built Around Flesh

Inside this body
old sidewalk buckles, the wind
hurls the rain because it can,

strikes the gravel I've filched
from playgrounds and hardwoods
beguiled once again into ghosting

their leaves. It's true,
if not verisimilar, except
those days that privilege

orange pylons, the jack-
hammer driving its snout
into the road. Besides a couple

of succulent approximations,
the paddocks where we put
the extra princes, the acne

on the mannequin, the urn,
most of what continues
will diminish, tangle

or accelerate, even
the Maker in process, half-
naked in His closet and

deliberating over which
cuff links will look best
at the millennium bash.

Cities built around branches
built around flesh, built
with a howl and a yawp.

Like the others I wait my turn
for the signal, those radiant
pummelings, the gumption to heat

the last crucifix and cauterize
my ambivalence. What's the plan
if we miss the hors d'oeuvres?

Before the walnuts, the maples,
the locusts, the oaks, the sycamores
go first. How astonishing

you've offered to give me,
my friend, the sleekest
and thickest of ropes.

Seneca

Here you can release
all the words you shouldn't
have risked, the things
you didn't do, watch
hummingbirds spin amid

geraniums, purple martins jet
from the boathouse to the lake.
A few days and you'll unstick
all your humid attitudes,

and if not, then idle down
to the lacquer, the pine, each
ambitious nail hammered
through the deck. Meanwhile,
the gods continue to lift

their cumulus barbells
up and over the western
hills. Let them strain. Let
them sweat. How sweet

to avoid any such work.
When we dive into this water,
cobalt, windblown, fierce,
we're certain to come out
on the other side of yes.

Ontario

The earth chooses to keep
this lake in its pocket.
Plastic shovel and a pail, our kids
prefer Wednesday to paradise.
But only for a while. So often

confused, the wind thinks it pushes
the sun off the tips of crests.
Crayfish in the muck below me
yank transparent threads
and I roll from my stomach

to my back, drift and scoop
clear apostrophes of water. Once
upon a time. . . . In the beginning. . . .
There is another language
we almost speak, the brave

resilience of widows
who leave the names
of their husbands in telephone books,
the understated confidence
of the little men appointed

to the planning board, almost
a whisper, a bellow, a song.
See how the salt-and-pepper clouds
shake reluctant droplets
over breakwalls and piers,

the sails of yachts dragging
their wakes like run-on sentences.
The things that are restless
in ourselves will rattle
through our children far away

from here, without
ambivalence or faith. Once
upon a time. . . . In the beginning. . . .
Why bother to challenge
the waves, feed the rocks

vagabonding to shore.
There is another language
difficult to fathom.
This is why I roll, I drift
until water weeds grow from my arms.

Saranac

What's good about water,
motorboats and docks can be
delicious when few people
are near. Birches that lean
crooked trunks have long since

issued their leaves to the lake.
Pickerel zip winter parkas
around themselves and sink.
Canoes racked. Skis mounted
in the boathouse safe

from the chop of November.
Still here. Still here—
two lights in the kitchen
windows of the cottage
off the point. What pleasure

to elbow a table, peacock
three aces, a pair of jacks,
drink scotch, crunch pretzels
and burp. No summer folk,
only the men who wait

these sluggish hours, hand after
hand, for dawn, the buck
that walks through the shallows.
Hope is anyone's guess. Maybe
the moon will hang its hat

in the pines on the eastern ridge.
Maybe a little sleet or maybe not,
this moment balanced amid
almost and was, now that words
call the bluff of their meanings,

and each wife left alone
under heavy blankets moistens
in her sleep. Look how the flush
withstands the straight
for six dollars and fifty cents.

There's the ruckus of water
against rocks, the smell of tobacco
and spruce, the thought of men
doing nothing useful in a world
so weary of usefulness.

Wherever the Wander Leads

opposable thumbs won't save us from ourselves
though they've helped exaggerate the drama sliding
toward denouement without free overdraft protection

only therapists and bomb-sniffing dogs, three months
or three thousand miles, whichever comes first.
Opposable thumbs won't save us from ourselves

as your toddler shuffles in, lifts up the sheet and asks
his mommy if he can have a chipmunk, too. Little people
don't care about free overdraft protection, oblivious

each whenever contains its own history, bootcrunch
and snort, the ding, ding, ding of the microwave warming
opposable thumbs that won't save us from ourselves,

the swollen grapes blowing autumn down the river
through the village, those diligent shops and steeples,
the promise of free overdraft protection, ibid., ergo,

ad infinitum. . . . Let the poem fracture prosody,
the tonic go flat, opposable thumbs won't save us
from ourselves, the office file crammed

with spooky government forms. Why live in the stable
of free overdraft protection, or beneath a rainbow
whose confidence is impressive but misplaced. If nothing

else, we know how to somersault, how to bounce.

Cycling Through Taylor's Basin

I am spinning toward Rudy's
Salvage Shop, toward the Western
Methodist Church, crab apple, some
brick homes with wrap-around
porches. A man I do not know

moves a rake over his yard, building
small campfires of leaves.
He stops and waves, his three kids
zigzag across the lawn in new sneaks.
Cut wood. Rope swing. Wheelbarrow.

I love this hamlet, all the people
who hitch rumpled husks
of corn to their screens, satisfied
to let the sun work their clothes
while the flicker clacks in the oak.

Like anyone else, I need to travel
among the old versions of who
we thought we were
before each of us adopted
the pious and pernicious,

those ways sure to leave
some blatant mark of how
we wanted this, demanded that.
And so it's good to smell
woodsmoke, the cut pumpkins,

hear the Labrador bark.
I wave back with the next gear shift
as these kids spill through russet piles,
laugh, roll and kick, oblivious
of their father, his plastic rake,

the blue velocity of my bike,
the dozen gravestones across the road
without flowers, mottled, cracked,
leaning north and south, but mostly
toward each other.

Third Night in San Francisco

Margaritas, Cheese Doodles, Alfred Hitchcock
and a futon. Such an excellent quartet
though it failed to keep them awake.
His snore: repeated tugs on the outboard's rope.
Hers: the sudden whistle telling sperm
free swim is up. What's left of the cake
squats in the fridge. Avoiding slick maneuvers
the tabby leaps to the counter, starts in
on a puddle of triple sec. And why not.
He's the big kahuna. When the geography of place
sublets the geography of distance, the mind
becomes a carnival of fabulous assumptions,
the cat would say if he could talk.
Paper lanterns and trolleys, a few boxes
still sluggish with fog. Like most newlyweds
they haven't decided anything close to essential:
who's in charge of the transitive verbs?
Is that a hunch about the future or a frothy glass
of nonchalance? And while they slumber
beneath the television's bloated eye, a pack
of lukewarm angels slop paint on the walls
at Alcatraz, deface the murals of North Beach,
struck by the happy notion to strafe the Cadillacs
on The Bay Bridge, push the teeth of divine
chain saws through the voluminous cable, following
their instincts to promote a little commotion,
achieve results that domino through the night
with the effortless power of human muscle,
the way he coughs and throws an arm against
her breast, which makes the clitoris flutter.

It's only reflex, the cat would say if he could talk.
How despite their promises, vitamins collapse
and most relatives don't help, the angels carving
scores of obscenities and idols into the bricks
at Union Square, howling through the Tenderloin,
lobbing cigarette butts into Aquatic Park, any stunt
to abate this eternal boredom which exceeds all
suffering they weathered in the flesh, when they too
welcomed the pleasures of monoglycerides and tequila,
like these newlyweds entwined in a rhythm
of snore and turn, turn and snore, the perfect
vulnerability of sleep, exhausted lovers of whom
it could be said know nothing of what follows
this third night in San Francisco, the geography
of place, the geography of distance. And yet
if they find themselves in search of guidance
let's hope they think to look beyond the advice
of eager siblings and parents, neighbors and angels,
toward the constant rhythm of crest and break, break
and crest that is the work of famished heart, voracious
heart, engorging heart, heart-sated heart, the pulse
of this moonlit ocean outside their apartment,
where, even after millions of years, every possible
intrusion and burdensome pressure, a whole lot of water
still finds itself married to a whole lot of salt.

Vitamins or Nautilus

Because he refused to lob each opponent
smothered the net, cut the angles
still available to him after fifty-eight years.

Not that his wife admonished such tactics.
She cared little for fresh balls, though, at times,
helped position ice packs on a swollen foot.

During the cookout or while nephews tore
the wrapping from presents he felt his exuberance
deflate. Even as a boy he never challenged

the neighborhood bully, seldom thought about
the benefits of ambush. Aristocratic decorum,
he once read in a book. Did she sense this?—

pushing his rebuttal off course like a freighter
rolled by whitecaps. Well, they'd be at the Cape
in a few days. Joyce flouncing across the deck,

new pumps and her polka dot skirt, and Mike
bashing woods through the fairway, punching irons.
Somehow it mattered less, as he watched

the bubbles in his drink and the sugary dunes,
that his putts were short, how he always folded
with two pair. The hermit crab sliced

by the crane's beak was another sadness that forgot
the freedom of limits. Yet, if his assumptions
were flawed, maybe vitamins or Nautilus, those tapes

guaranteed to expand the abbreviated
parts of oneself. Then again, why bother.
Such efforts seemed partly inane, could swamp

the relationships buoyed by a long-standing truce.
Let others attempt that whole vision thing, perhaps
locate new types of blindness, the equivalent
of Quakers holding candles in a lighthouse.

Having Evolved from Grass

our eyes seesaw green,
go chartreuse into hazel, umber
edged by saffron and dun.

At home our kids
guzzle cloudbursts of milk,
thicken in spurts, at school

wave their arms to become
fields of windblown wheat,
trusting they have the answer,

something of the fluid plant
that enables each of us
to yield, acquiesce without

indignation, be it clippers,
pesticides, the implacable herd. . . .
Most of who we are

does not blaze or spangle,
rarely scatters a redolent brume.
From grass it's understood

what matters most is not
showing off but showing up,
breaching what we can—

asphalt, gravel, brick,
one among so many, this
our constant work and harder.

Now That You've Anchored

the ship of yourself in the port of your college dorm,
who's going to yank the sheet from the mattress,
click the nubs of new bicuspids,
if you're not around to dream?

When your dolls escape into their miniskirts,
and the night improvises on its black guitar,
who'll be left to ask for water, have to pee,
have to pee and ask for water?

Now whose friends will want to sleep over?
(while the rest of us are sleeping with).
Bunk beds, big plans, all that teeter-totter chatter,
who's going to fart, guffaw and giggle,
need one more blanket, five more minutes, please?

When the subs dive, the searchlights flare,
and our doors, half-open, suddenly close,
who's going to be in the next room snoring?—
a few mumbles, an occasional grunt,
so we'll know what is safe and what is here.

II

Moonfabulousmoonfib

> *"When she was full—nights as bright as day,*
> *but with a butter-colored light—it looked as if*
> *she were going to crush us; when she was new,*
> *she rolled around the sky like a black umbrella*
> *blown by the wind."*
> —Italo Calvino

The vagabond moon drops a pebble in his shoe, picks
up pylons along the road and builds
an orange pyramid. We should be conscious

of no more grass than will cover our graves,
says the vagabond moon, his voice a tuba floating
in a glass of milk, a glass of milk floating

down the vas deferens. Life jackets optional,
says the vagabond moon, but everyone must wear
their euphemisms. A million tow trucks and a single

parking meter—sweetness, did you leave enough
change? Are you still afraid of the asteroid forest
or will you loan him your knapsack of stars?

* * *

Listen: the Milky Way is the flawless whisker of God,
and each of the stars in the Pleiades illuminates
a family value. Fundamentalist moons understand this,

argue that even delinquent comets can be saved.
How to anticipate those acts, benign at first,
which will occupy us more than they should.

Press your ear against the only book, what
you label the big bang is the sound of woman
being snapped from Adam's rib, the reptilian hiss

of nebulae. Though orbits take us toward apogee
we are forever close to Him, Alpha and Omega,
who makes righteous converts of abandoned debris.

*   *   *

Red-faced as the light refracted from an eclipse,
the kindergarten moon flings a dirty snowball and shouts,
Comet! comet! Galileo is smart enough to place him

in time-out with Heraclitus and Ptolemy. Was it parents
or the firepricks of the zodiac that showed us how
to mollify our kids through selective concessions?

Just look at the craters his tempests produce, these
luminous hints and fresh approximations. All we want
is a week to catch our breath, dual hammocks,

a pitcher of lemonade along the Mare Tranquillitatis.
Clandestinely, the telephone poles pass notes from school
to school. If he apologizes, go ahead and let him out.

*   *   *

Balance is never stillness only continual flows
of adjustment, frappé or liquefy, the anorexic moon
scrambles constellations into frothy elements, dreams

her waxing figure without earthshine, that stout
pallid glow. How long will NASA nourish the obsolete
Astrochimps? You and I on the lawn by the big

yellow house, our trusty telescope. Neptune is a dollop
of confectionery sugar, Ganymede a brussels sprout.
Who's to say what's reasonable, what's dangerous?

Like Joan of Arc she hears voices, the echoes
that forget their feet, her cycle suspended pours
the mix down a bottomless, gravitational sink.

★   ★   ★

Beneath the weight of escarpments and cliffs
of solid ice, Charon tells Pluto, Love me black as I am,
when I'm white everyone will love me, condemned

as they are to such freedom. Existentialist moons
create the story of themselves, how the impact spills
molten balls into space. Be authentic. Be responsible.

Don't rely on thermonuclear fusion, the energy delivered
by gamma rays. We've plenty of chutzpah to balance
the pianist's light touch, the prostate's strangle hold,

and autocrats will never think to extradite us
if we hide between saliva and the Elvis stamp.
Once again Charon cries, I cannot wax, I'll wax.

* * *

Shock waves and surface quakes, every so often
the linebacker moon flexes his mascons, thumps
our little spacecraft into various orbits.

All this language we suit up and send out
on the field, green syllables undercut by perception.
Four billion years of practice and these planets

still refuse to huddle. He can't wait for them,
for the chance to demolish some pompous meteorite,
roll about in the blood and the mud, yes,

in the blood and the mud roll about. And you and I?
Well, just because we're given kneecaps and knuckles
doesn't mean they'll stick around until the end of the game.

* * *

Why brood about image?—most of the universe
is nonluminous matter. Though try to convince
adolescent moons of black holes beyond themselves,

how Saturn never clipped rings to his nose, that
Olympus Mons is a mountain, not a rock group.
Reluctant or zealous, we grope across the attic

of someone else's emotions, their happiness heaped
over copious pain. Babycakes, you're confusing sunspots
with zits. Don't fret. I'm sure he'll call tonight.

What's news but the rumors snubbing wanna-be gossip,
letter M for magnetic, mercurial lust, the tridents
these callow moons pitch into each other's crusts.

* * *

Getting there from someplace else on vitamins and luck
puts us at the mercy of ecumenical dogma, cosmic
reactionaries. The best alternative, say Unitarian moons,

Is another task force that will impart enough space
for each asterism and support those bodies bruised
by meteor showers or suffering from chemical imbalance.

The Galactic Interfaith Committee suggests we recognize
Indonesian and Chinese satellites, World Federation
        Wrestling,
the seven iron Alan Shepard left in his bag. Please

open your lunar hymnals to the page you identify with.
The choir will sing the first verse; we will join them
on the refrain. As always, feel free to whistle or hum.

* * *

Viet Nam was about tungsten, school yard alliances
about force. The soldier moon is trained to grasp
these things, and how noble campaigns often finish

like the crows mobbing rooftops at dusk. Wallop
Jupiter with shrapnel, drive a bayonet through Mars.
Should we court-martial the truth for breaking rank

or should we decorate its bodyguard of lies?
At the moment the walls refuse their clocks,
the soldier moon forges a letter to his wife,

carries out his charge. While you and I sit down
with anonymous diplomats, deliberate
over salmon and claret, almost, maybe and perhaps.

*   *   *

Each star ends in a supernova, approaches Wagner,
Beethoven's ninth. But the virtuoso moon avoids
such pyrotechnics. She alone rises new at sunset,

goes full at dawn, fashions sublime grace notes
for the fugue of the universe. Rosin and bow,
where ideal solutions exist, problems cease,

the rest of us doomed to regurgitate the chart's
popular hits while memory murders surprise.
Photographs from Voyager, spectroscopic readings,

why all the fuss to find liquid water beyond
planet earth? Can't you hear the virtuoso moon?
To lose one's identity is to find lost music.

*   *   *

Though we've wheelchaired a multitude of robust
fables from the infirmary of the imagination
they rarely make the air waves or history books,

and all maria on the convalescent moon go by Palus
Epidemiarum. Why be shocked. There's no vaccine
to inoculate us from the Marsh of Epidemics

which each autumn the politicians drag us through.
Better to live within the wound, among the bolides
and planetesimals, Venus a lonesome greenhouse

that went crazy on itself, carbon dioxide, pressure
and heat, the syntax of a brilliant suffocation—
What more could we desire? says the convalescent moon.

*   *   *

Haloed in smoke, the executive moon drinks
from a bottle exhausted with vapor and salt,
a few muffled phonemes outside the click

of bicuspids, the look of a woman swigging beer,
that coy and casual glance, a crater from which
we cannot scale and so open our billfolds

toward the profiles of dead presidents,
as the moon with its elbows on mahogany calls
for another shot, removes its cuff links

amid the pulse of fireflies over opulent ports,
the brothels where we sleep, famished and sated,
with our gibbous flesh, our slivered hearts.

We Cannot Buy Cliffs Notes

for something like theodicy, how to crack an egg
and slurp the yoke, rebuke a clump
of presumptuous grass. It's not easy
to negotiate the dirt catacombs cut
by rodents, to distinguish camouflage
from talisman now that they've removed
those Burma Shave signs along the highway
leaving us slick topography maps, the binoculars'
black funnels. Look: is that a meadowlark
or the brilliant et cetera of our doubt?
Insurance agents who classify natural disasters
Acts of God should be handcuffed and escorted
to seminary. Carrot peelings atop the spinach,
the colon's little broom has been busy, busy
since Maximus declared the line is a function
of metabolism. Each deal umpteen strings attached,
but are they threads or monkey ropes? Pop
the trigger and the recoil from a Nitro Express
will make your cerebellum bounce against your skull.
Maybe the Greeks were addicted to connecting-the-dots
and so scratched their fictions into the vacant
sky; maybe the gargoyles have always
split the bread, blessed the wine;
when you and I reach the bottom of the slope
maybe the most intelligent choice
is to drag our sleds back up
for another swift and scary ride.

Joseph and the Boss

Pharaoh, it seems, has a bad case
of nocturnal bovine vision. He's also dogged
by phantom ears, though not the sort
that flank the head and make it look
like a taxi with its doors flung open,
but the farm variety type jammed
into the earth from Egypt to Damascus.
Today, he's exhausted—a mess of nerves
and sockets, feeling rotten about his choice
to nix the baker and the prospect
of unraveling such ludicrous dreams;
therefore, in this morning's dull haze,
summons a scribe, outlaws meat loaf, corn oil,
pillows and quilts, those gaunt subjects
with incessant appetites. Court magicians
toss pebbles in the dirt, scratch their pates.
He wants answers and quick, but it's a good
three thousand years until Sigmund releases
the disguised fulfillments of the ego's
repressed wishes from his dazzling medicine bag.
(Another decade on top of that before Carl
jumps up and down, shouting—No penis, no penis,
it's collective unconscious!) Meanwhile,
Pharaoh's so tired we've booked the odds
he'll trade the Sphinx for a Sominex. Of course,
that pharmaceutical and the yellow sedans,
(check the reference above), operated
by his progeny and racing through places
yet to be discovered (Newark, the Bronx),
aren't available unless he steals

the Hebrew's formula to masticate time.
Which returns us to the topic: who are the players?
what are the stakes? There's our big man
with little shut-eye and lots of royal angst
trapped among a bunch of worthless factotums,
including the lucky butler with his grape-spackled
lips, Jacob staring at the robe, Pot'i-phar howling
at his wife, eleven brothers running flocks
across the desert, while the dude they sold
to some Ishmaelites hangs out in a dungeon,
like his Pharaoh also dreams of cows munching cows
who become ketchup, relish, onion rolls and cups
of fresh lemonade, potato salad, watermelon
and dozens of rhubarb pies all swirled
in pulsing, diaphanous colors.
But then there's this: unlike the Boss
he's not vexed by premonitions of losing exports
or real estate, that's why our naked fantast
goes on sleeping among the roaches and the mold,
the mildew and the rats, he slumbers
and slumbers well. Because it's easy to relinquish
those possessions they strip from you
if you believe you're the propane for God's barbecue.

Poof

So what if her sex life was a slow train
that only stopped in dilapidated towns.
By removing the variable of expectation
she still managed a formula in the neighborhood
of science. Perhaps beef stroganoff
was the highest art, and guys lacking
status or wealth made an effort to acknowledge
overt deficiencies, fell toward little fibs
rather than big lies, the syntax of their affection
a dangling participle. It seemed that every wife
who suddenly chose to drip across the deck
of some playboy's yacht, bikini and coconut oil,
was diluted by insolence, the bogus rush
of diving into the shallow end.
How else to explain Veronica?—her steamy fling
with the venture capitalist from Amherst,
cut short by a road sign gusting
through the Ferrari's glass, only hours
after administering (what her sated friend called)
masterful cunnilingus. He died under the weight
of: *Entering Lowell.* The absence of evidence
no proof of the evidence of absence, nor help
to a woman, this same friend, on the phone,
her anguish accelerating into denial and rage,
all those demonstrative junctures,
as she played confidant and shrink, recalling
the other gift of memory is to forget,
how the boots of anxiety and doubt
walk us toward a place where even the reverse
has a reverse. And when Veronica

loosed everything that needed expulsion,
the episode finished or suspended, the cradle
again found its receiver, the comforting click
of yin and yang, she returned
to slicing mushrooms, thinking about Ralph,
how he slept by the fridge, a lump of reticent
fur, how cats, even the males, understood
the perpetual delight found in the aloof,
while we humans throw punches at the cosmos,
a magnificent fuss, liposuction and dental work,
hoopla, flimflam, scuttlebutt, exhausted by our own
verbosity, and then one day poof!—
we're gone. If those are the stakes, she thought,
why not grant each other the illusion of value
like surgeons introducing themselves at cocktail parties,
or get the occasional hump from a tone-deaf
bassoonist, a corpulent jock. As long as a few
creative ideas refused to atrophy
among the dreck, and that they recognize
the potential of homemade stroganoff, she'd entertain,
at least for the rest of this month,
whoever stumbled in, bad ties, bad breath,
the most gloriously useless and beautiful men.

Viagra Falls

From the precipice we watch
the loaded boat rumble toward
the cataract, brume glazing the gold
slickers of those on deck. Eroticism
is experiment, constant variation, a thirst
for otherness, the body at play.
Keep in mind, gentlemen, our tour guide adds,
lip gloss and painted nails, the florid
VF embroidered on her blouse,
Dog-humping sex is always the same.
Poets and libertines, the rich, the pickpockets,
rabbis and pimps, attorneys and thugs,
those puckishly faithful and those
repressed, the epicureans, the anchorites,
bureaucrats and stoics, the licentious and discreet,
along with so many others, our tour guide says,
who's provided insights on *Daphnis and Chloe*,
The Song of Songs, *Casablanca*. These men
below us ride *The Maid* toward the chance
to recover virility, the lost equipment
that once enhanced the erotic.
We watch the boat cut engines and idle
near the falls as reckless gusts
toss seagulls and scatter cologne.
Each of them has to be intrepid,
our tour guide says, who for lunch ate
tunafish on toast, a sleek Popsicle.
Heart attack and stroke, mixed with nitrates
the blood pressure drops, and sometimes
the phallus cramps which results in long-term

damage. Yes, there've been casualties,
but we're not liable. They've signed the papers,
read the print. We gaze a final time
at the distant boat, only half
of what it was, the mist now swallowing
its stern. The erotic is a rhythm
that transforms and diverts sex
from the purpose of reproduction
and returns us to reconciled nature,
what's left of paradise. But before all that,
our tour guide adds, holding up
a baby blue diamond between her thumb
and index finger, You may require
the assistance only we can provide
if your equipment starts to fail,
your wife gets disgruntled, your girlfriend
or partner start to talk about
subordinate performance, about dating
other people, which, considering
everything else at stake,
is the wrong option, because this
is Viagra Falls, the body's seventh wonder
with a full money-back guarantee,
and like these men below us
you too can summon the courage
to recover lost strength, your portion
of the erotic, that portion you deserve.
Why not book passage on *The Maid*
and do it soon, because, gentlemen,
after numerous studies and millions
of dollars, medical experts have deduced
this little pill's only as powerful
as the water you take it with.

After Decades of Silence, Toilet Speaks

Last things first.
In regard to the great
nocturnal-diurnal conflict
prompting all that disaffection,
resentment and grief, you must understand—
I don't care if the seat is up or down.
And though you've brought many parts of yourself,
not once have you brought a gift, ribbons and bow,
some small token of thanks
for each brilliant thought you've hatched
while resting much flesh on my porcelain
which is not a hole in the ground.
It's one of the responsibilities of art
to provide others with more intelligent
questions, the flash of synchronic time.
I have no such charge, yet
when you need me, really need me,
even more than love's orifice,
there's nothing else you desire.
Look how the planets and satellites float
in the night's black bowl. Does it startle you
that I can be romantic? Whatever the occasion,
some people love to booze and schmooze.
Some don't. But everyone visits me,
even those who bluster cheap euphemisms,
though, in truth, I exceed metaphor.
Toilet is toilet as death is death,
so many parts of yourself
whooshed away. I know you mostly avoid
ambivalence and solitude, won't admit

you're still perplexed by how the flapper
and lift chain work. Have another drink,
another snack. You can't stop philosophy
from conceding metaphysics to science—
splash, splash, flush—the universe expands,
brain cells burn while something like the truth
plays hide-and-go-seek. I'm here. Always here.
My perfect ellipse stays put.

The Ineffable

Of course it's the moment
all lovers hope to reach
between cigarettes and the work
of each other's buttons.

In nursery school
you hung out with its pals
enchantment and *wonder*,
stacked blocks, spread paint.

After the explosion, the sweep
of bullets through the market,
it takes up shop in your throat.
Looks like you were lucky

enough to survive the errant
missile. Grab a chair, my friend,
the one covered with dust,
and it will buy you a drink.

Oh, yes, did I mention?—
the hole in the rope
from which the body dangles,
the gaze of an ape.

Poem Without a Freight Train or a Pocket Watch

As their modesty now proved bothersome
Johnny pawned his box of fabulous lasts.
Each insight contains its own special blindness,
and all the little firsts came shrieking out.

Johnny pawned his box of fabulous lasts.
The heart is torn between practice and theory,
and all the little firsts come shrieking out.
Like some clouds we're just necessarily mistaken.

The heart is torn between practice and theory,
those sharp brilliances the violin kaleidoscopes.
Like some clouds we're just necessarily mistaken.
What's a horse but a mule with a marketing team.

Those sharp brilliances the violin kaleidoscopes.
Susie touched the cardboard, sent a razor through the tape.
What's a horse but a mule with a marketing team.
Knock, knock, who's there?—the ampersands of fear.

Susie touched the cardboard, sent a razor through the tape
while we chose sides and adopted bogus rules.
Knock, knock, who's there?—the ampersands of fear,
that poem without a freight train or a pocket watch.

While we chose sides and adopted bogus rules
Johnny pawned his box of fabulous lasts.
Eyes tossed from their sockets and nipples bloated
all the little firsts came shrieking out.

What'll It be Tonight, the Heart or the Fist?

White bucks and white smock, ecstasy arrives.
Legalists scatter, hide behind hailstones,
outside and within the language facade.
We get the ears the wind lifts from the flowers.

Legalists scatter, hide behind hailstones,
the match and its tiny speech of smoke.
Outside and within the language facade
we draw these pictures on a slab of light.

The match and its tiny speech of smoke.
Be afraid of the pungent and the odorless.
We draw these pictures on a slab of light.
Always the mind follows itself following itself.

Be afraid of the pungent and the odorless.
Has the blackboard put out a contract on the chalk?
Always the mind follows itself following itself,
most of our efforts disturbingly comfortable.

Has the blackboard put out a contract on the chalk?
Let's pull over the view and take a look at the car.
Most of our efforts disturbingly comfortable,
friends, what'll it be tonight, the heart or the fist?

Let's pull over the view and take a look at the car
as legalists scatter, hide behind hailstones.
White bucks and white smock, ecstasy arrives.
We get the ears the wind lifts from the flowers.

Poetry Is a Game of Managing Your Mistakes

the body a pair of galoshes drying in the corner,
sluggish with compliance and doubt, aversions and desires.
I love the dirt she packs inside the little clay pots,
those dank clumps of soil that eventually we'll join.

Sluggish with compliance and doubt, aversions and desires,
each syllable is a closed door and a passage through.
I love the dirt she packs inside the little clay pots,
such gorgeously abrupt and subordinate blossoms.

Each syllable is a closed door and a passage through.
There's less time to think about languid elopements,
such gorgeously abrupt and subordinate blossoms.
You get nothing if your arms remain crossed.

There's less time to think about languid elopements,
our awkward attempts to stitch the cloak of forbearance.
You get nothing if your arms remain crossed.
Just imagine the visions O'Keeffe had during cunnilingus.

Our awkward attempts to stitch the cloak of forbearance.
We've been assigned these vital, insignificant parts.
Just imagine the visions O'Keeffe had during cunnilingus.
Like marriage, poetry's a game of managing your mistakes.

We've been assigned these vital, insignificant parts.
The body that pair of galoshes drying in the corner.
What's cleverness but a fresh symptom of heart disease,
which brings us back, as it always does, to dank clumps of soil.

Do Something Useful

my wife says and often, though she
should know better as I've always
lacked the moxie, the toolbox talent
of the men who rebuild engines,

solder pipes, fix cantankerous
appliances and understand how most
thingamajigs work. Such guys
don't need manuals, assembly instructions.

Like Achilles they've been dipped
in a river of turpentine. What
every woman wants, they can accomplish:
drywall, staple gun, the thrill of the bolt

entering the nut. Do something useful.
The shingles are warped, the windowpanes
shot. She's right, yet ought to recall
there's the strength of envisioning

a predicament past its trouble,
the raw intelligence that lets one part
locate another, et cetera, et cetera.
Simply put: you possess such force

or you don't. Darling, let's be blunt.
When it comes to home repairs
there's nothing mythic about me, nothing
Hephaestian like my neighbors, who forge

their own shields and while the arrows
pop and Troy smolders, I miss
all the action for I am incapable
of sawing my way out of the horse.

When We Lie Down Beneath Vanilla Wood

S is the shape that never dissolves,
a molten trumpet, a plastic

octopus. Did you learn these moves
filming acrobats? Such bones

seem more essential than stars. It helps
to be fluid and somewhat tenacious.

Think of ants crossing the road.
Let's order adjectives at brunch. Thanks

for the kiss and the work you've done
to save me from a job with my name on my shirt.

Having Evolved from Stones

we honor patience, those
who ignore gossip.
Crouching among the familiar,
we watch for erosions, take

the necessary precautions
not to expose ourselves.
We know the blind crawlers
who bump against us,

birds scratching our scalps,
the smell of swamp milkweed,
fresh manure, how the frost
ties its crystal mantilla. . . .

Our men boast of their strength
and heft. Clairvoyant,
our women sense tremors
long before the quake.

Having evolved from stones
there's no need to dwell
on the inevitable—
the plough will scrape, the snow

cover. Somewhere
we decided to stop
asking wherefore and how,
saved our hands to grasp

what earth we can,
quaff rain, eat wind, welcome
the roots of frail saplings
brushing our feet.

Such Family, Such Yule

After the goose, sweet potatoes
and stuffing, she calls us to the pedal
organ. *Adeste Fideles. Gloria in Excelsis.*

We push carols through the cracks
in the fireplace bricks. Dad's
on the wrong verse. Aunt Sarah's

a notch flat. Determined, we continue
while Grandma covers us,
crescendos and thick chords,

the melody glissading
across the treble clef. Wasn't it
Brueghel who said he didn't care

about the God in man,
just the man in God? And aren't
his rustics much like us?—

goiter and wart, cataract
and scar, the mottled irons
near the fire, a wedge of curd

on a board and a host of other
miraculous imperfections. Why not
praise them as we might the canvas

or the hairs in the brush, our valiant
disintegrating voices. It's what we have
and we're not so badly off. Tonight

we'll sing down snow, sing the sharp
needles from the tamarack.
Hark the Herald. Joy to the World

where doubters and believers
can dent every note
all the difficult way to paradise and back.

III

Unfazed by Velocities or Agendas

he read it straight, he read it drunk, he read it stoned—
the night's milky-narrative of stars, those distant
triangles with their gorgeous, terrifying hearts.

The task is to abandon your animal self,
forget the treasure maps where why replaces x.
He read it straight, he read it drunk, he read it stoned.

Each morning trouble gets up earlier than me,
makes few decisions. Should I put on fresh socks?—
or triangles with their gorgeous, terrifying hearts.

We continue to pretend we are mostly satisfied.
Mostly satisfied, we continue to pretend.
He read it straight, he read it drunk, he read it stoned.

The phenomenal is a loan with hefty interest.
Who looks in the mirror to see the mirror—
past the triangles with their gorgeous, terrifying hearts.

Don't worry if the plot ends up misplaced, the climax
botched. These characters will just keep on talking,
triangles with their gorgeous, terrifying hearts.
Read it straight. Read it drunk. Read it stoned.

Questions for Prufrock

Do you know where to find
a moon without a planet,

a god without a loneliness?
When will the rain take off it shoes?

Why won't the language we think
in our heads give itself up

to pencil and paper? What's the ratio
of gas to oil in your basic heart?

Who put you in charge of imitating,
much less stealing? How long

before we gain admittance
to the Museum of Come-and-Go?

Do mermaids bury their bones?

What Happens Without Fanfare

at our cottage on the lake
happens because we're lucky
and the deck chairs recline,
owes little to the sleek

geometry the spider left
in the enervated boat. Dime novel
and strawberry lip gloss,
sunglasses parked on the bridge

of her nose. When the wind
starts to gust a thousand cattails
yield. Down and up, down and up,
like Muslims facing Mecca. Our lives

a curious mix of irony and hymn.
How implausible that it's us
watching waves slither past
the world we thought recalcitrant, sure.

Dragonflies mount, unhinge
themselves. Another gust
and the cattails flex. Soon we will eat
the pickerel gasping in the sink.

Harvest Festival, Tahaughnik, New York

Stopping the stroller he looks at his watch
and says, I believe it's now officially
beer-thirty. And though nostalgia
is often dubious, you'll have those suds
with your just-arrived-from-Ohio brother,
perhaps on a picnic bench under maples,
while the wind's ball of twine
unravels in your pocket, whips about
a village with so much to follow—
fast kids and white hots, streets
full of amateur musicians and clowns,
the smell of crushed apples among
the knickknack booths, the bloated
pumpkins beside the tractors,
pinwheels and ice cream, the vegetable
wagons parked on the lawn near the statue
of the intrepid war hero. Anyone
can feel local, pluck a grape from the crust
of a homemade pie, twirl what's left
of a purple-belled gentian. Scholars agree
the Iroquois spoke a word which translated
means *intricate balance*. We know that.
Most of us taciturn, then suddenly convivial,
hoping our entrances won't lack the spunk
of each departure, something like the robust,
tumbling sparrows, or the thought
before such thoughts which assume
the flavor of happiness. Accordingly,
we're clothed for the go-anywhere-ramble,
husbands, wives and children, our favorite

sneaks or shoes finding new ways to disperse
little eskers of leaves, the sharp, tenacious rasp
of mid-October that makes you realize
how much you gain from these spontaneous
opportunities for purposeless fun, how the heart
will let itself become that cup of beer
you hand to a stranger, video camera and a map
of festival exhibits, who's also stopped
to catch his breath and gape at the rumpled earth
buttressing the valley and the brook, lean against
the generous frame of a combine harvester, as if
he'd spent all day gathering wheat, threshing chaff,
as if this was the only place called home.

Cross-Country, Gershwin, Pizza

Look: when people wonder if it's the going out
or the coming back, if the flakes are brisk
as clarinet notes and the crust tolerates our heft,

so many dark loquacious olives, recall that truth
is always dubious compared to fiction
and troubadours without irony turn quixotic places

lethal. Realize you might be the woman who panics
and rings the fire department that upon arrival
learns the red-tangerine is not the adjacent house

in flames, but the start of another sunblast
through which the piano counterpoints, syncopates
while anchovies fling gossip about the mozzarella.

Most often subterfuge is only method acting,
this hour like a good bottle of wine, a little more
than both of us need and almost enough

if opened with friends. We might as well let
arthritis meet wisdom, acquiesce to the poles
puncturing snow, the skis pushing themselves
over miles of frosted earth—yes no   yes no   yes no

Though Monarchs Exploit the Disparity Among Us

more often than not a little booze is the great equalizer.
Rum that dark window at the back of our heads.
How long before the waitress returns with the drinks?

At each party there's a guy reluctant to speak.
When he finally starts talking, he never quits—
tequila, tequila. Booze the great mystifier.

Glasses filled with double malt and bourbon, those
cold spots in the lake that startle your legs.
How long before they issue different life preservers?

A woman and her date salacious in the park,
eager to open bottles of imported beer. She strokes
but nothing happens. Booze the great nullifier.

A few cocktails, a couple shots and soon
we call upon embellished versions of ourselves.
How long before the audience escapes from the theater?

If you locate the vodka, take a gulp for Vladimir Ilyich,
Khrushchev and Stalin, bold Gorby who put them
on ice. Among rivals, a little booze is the great equalizer.
How long before the waitress returns with our drinks?

American Fragment

Nancy S. Graves' oil & crayon on canvas

The wind plops its ladder against the house
and blows milky songs across your hip
that trombones retrieve and echo off industrious

boats. The gods of dairy products once inhabited
this spot, left the charts they used to excavate
the Ruins of Nonchalant, the moxie to crack open

littlenecks and hazelnuts. *Translatus, translatus,*
let's disappear beneath the bashful scarecrows
of hanging folders. When the southpaw thumps

the slugger on the head, how soon the romantic
becomes the self-righteous. Why not create promotions
for bric-a-brac nobody wants. Because my tonsils

look like tractor tires my dentist has purchased
a dismemberment plan, and the sheriff who reads
to incarcerated mice does so in fleeced pajamas.

Ersatz or whiteout, I'll take whatever's possible,
though, honestly, I'd rather swap amino acids
and the fictions roped to the bill of a turbulent duck
who's memorized the postal zips of faraway folks.

August Evening, Bright Hill Farm

Up this glacial ridge I walk,
a few scattered boulders and oaks
doing their best to slingshot wind.
The moment my footfall spooks a buck
in the corn his antlers become parentheses,
his tail an exclamation point
beyond my sight which is weak
and unreliable. But why complain,
renounce surprise or disparage
the syntax of astonishment—
one leg, two legs, four.
Like animal brides we shift
and evade, when trapped
tease the moon from our bones,
a wickedly impossible endeavor
unless you're luck's little fool,
in search of phosphorescence without
the facts and its obdurate truth.
One leg, two legs, three now six.
What work is more imperative
than clouds eating sky?
I note that Some—gone patient long—
At length, renew their smile—
She may be right. And if she's not
we haven't lost much. There's still
tenacity in that some and these friends
who also walk past the boulders
and the oaks, the dark vocabulary
of grasses and the sleep of their fathers,
to gather on this ridge, hold a candle

and sing for blueberries and vetch,
woodchucks and wheat, the ink
at the tip of Emily's pen and the frost
on the glass of her bedroom windows,
the fear that is late and the grace
that is early, for a thousand twilight fables
we've lost or misremembered, and for those
that split the heart with joy.

When the Mother of the Bride Is Dying

what we might offer fails in words
and so disappears to where pale light enfolds

the trees on the hill, this yard, the white book
still wet with our names. Her hands take guest

after guest, each of us standing in polished shoes
trying to keep our thoughts on the notes

the quartet so generously provides and away
from the mother's wig, the future and all

its naked conjecture that is a disservice
to the affection of the groom's handshake,

the fresh flowers held by the bride
who smiles her daughter smile, blossom and bud.

What else can we do besides wait, shuffle in a line
past the wood pile, the shrubs, a little further

through the shadows to greet the abundance
of another hour, despite the raw indifference of life,

which, at least, from our perspective,
guest after guest, has failed to overwhelm

all of their laughter, all of this love.

At the Department of Motor Vehicles

who you are and how you go merge,
but not before you wait it out
among plastic seats. There's
fresh wax on the floor,
some plants drooping brown
above each booth and a girl has bent
to the eye-test machine,
her butterscotch legs enough
to take you down the stupid roads of desire
until 158 is called. Such a number
is not likely to happen soon, and that's good—
you've stumbled into a poem
welcoming the not likely, the strange,
things disparate or black
at the bottom of the marsh,
tubas on leashes, porcupines
with cigarettes, the old
I-can't-believe-this-is-happening
as the pickup sweeps wide
and into your lane. . . .
Draw comfort from the theory
of a hundred billion stars,
the protracted sibilants
of background radiation, all those
supernovas blazing, galaxies
rushing off with their throttles
cranked, not likely to return.
Though the real work
is to hammer your own
assumptions toward the prospect

of raw insight, especially since
you habitually regurgitate
what others think. The man
in the seat to your right
continues to crack bubble gum.
Such rhythm is nothing less
than the play of brushes over snares.
Blue lights flash above each booth.
134, 135. Isn't eye test
another name for cosmic dwindle?—
hope a heavy foot and a full tank,
the possibility our Lord
will be grading on a curve.
If you slept here all week
you might end up cooking
for the woman who smiles
as she allots these numbers.
And when the forceps finally yank
your child out from under the hood
of her body, everything else
would fall into some kind
of lucid sequence,
and you'd understand
it's never about the urge
to make sense, to ask why,
only what you do with how you go,
this little, not likely existence
through which you so wondrously,
helplessly move—
green heart, yellow heart, green heart, red.

Cheesehead

                         Surely,
you wouldn't slab a piece
of cheddar to your pate,
tie it down like a bonnet, spend
all weekend in the library, the mall.
Think of myriad conversations—

depressed or elated,
fatigued, puzzled, even drunk,
not once did anyone say, not
at the office, the pharmacy,
not while making change, offering
directions, did anyone say—

I think I'll wear a Roquefort fedora,
and, you know, you'd look good
in a Limburger fez. Yet
here you are, shirtless at ten above,
the wind off the bay
in a safety blitz, your face

painted gold, forest green,
and on your head, yes, your noggin,
a wedge of synthetic cheese,
imitation fromage mass produced
at five cents a lick, marked up
to the eighteen bucks

you slapped down without shame
so you could stand among

thousands of folks crowned
with similar prefabricated molds,
stand and shout, taunt and curse,
choke down brats wrapped in onions,

slap hands, slurp beer, your gaze
fixed on a stretch of grass
where tiny men scramble,
smash against each other. . . .
E. M. Forster asserted
that the final test of a novel

will be our affection for it,
as it is the test of all things
we cannot define. Likewise
these cheeseheads, draped
with floppy banners, trinkets,
reeking of Pabst and hamburger grease.

Worn backwards they enervate
the opponent's offense, turned side-
ways help Favre pick apart
defensive schemes, and only
between quarters, or if the Pack's
notched thirty points

may cheeses be swapped, traded,
stripped from the head.
It's certain. No dog has ever
been so faithful, no car so
reliable as artificial curd.
And when, millennia from now,

others come upon the char, the rubble,
find a chunk, black and sodden,
wipe back the dust, surmise
that it was an icon
from the temple used to channel
great power, that its small

indentations were places
the gods could rest,
would they, these curious travelers
in helmets and uniforms,
would they be anything else
but converging on the truth?

Little Poem That Won't Go Away

Accept this story or I'll blow
you up. Accept this story
or I'll cut you down.

Bombs, guns and stories.
Stories, guns and bombs.
Each plosive a trigger,

each inflection a fuse.
Without desire the last
snowflakes erase the ones

before them, no argument
between the rain and the brook.
Bombs, guns and stories.

Stories, guns and bombs.
How insignificant compared
to the tantrums of stars,

the vanity of scrutable
truth. Even this poem
is a story you must never accept.

The Bible on the Counter
in Pat Verrazano's Paint Shop

is spackled with various acrylics,
 stays open
with the help of a stir stick

so that we can browse a passage
 or two, revisit
the feats of David and Moses,

the visions of Isaiah, though
 more often
than the prophets, I find myself

drifting toward Job. Virtuous,
 upright,
ever-fearful of God, each moment

cognizant that his wealth will increase
 if he makes
the proper offerings, if he's good

to his servants, respects the kids,
 his wife,
honors the work of his donkeys,

a hundred assiduous bulls.
 Job, whose life
has settled into itself like water,

the titanium dioxide in a gallon
        of Brilliant White
Semi-Gloss Latex Enamel, stain

resistant, covers any surface;
        lucky paint
that for years has reviewed the world

from a shelf high above the scrapers
        and drop cloths,
so many nervous little brushes. . . .

Of course, it's Yahweh's business,
        has been
since He opened shop in this stretch

of the universe, and He's a methodical
        persnickety owner,
keeps tabs on his inventory, rotates

stock, is known for his sudden
        liquidation sales.
And today is no exception—

He wants to move product, entice
        a few customers
with giveaways, perhaps some free

caulk to the next angel who floats in,
        which, turns out
to be the fallen day star himself,

in the middle of a job that requires
	sandpaper, sponges,
one gallon of paint. Any brand

will do. It doesn't matter,
	he says. They all
eventually buckle, inevitably crack.

Not this one, Yahweh answers,
	grabs a step
and reaches for the top shelf,

The Brilliant White Semi-Gloss
	Latex Enamel.
This one has always been different.

He descends the ladder, walks
	over to the table,
wedges the gallon into the mixer,

tightens each clamp. Add a thousand
	contaminants
and this paint will keep its color,

maintain its constant luminosity.
	Is that so,
Satan says, his eyes now locked

on the old bucket furiously shaking,
	his mind focused,
already priming the wager.

For Barbie, Who, After Much Vodka, to Celebrate Her Birthday, Spent the Night with Her Sister

Come back, please come back, my love,
to our ramshackle house and this powder
blue sky, the fat clouds above the fields,
the maples on fire, your fugitive gardens.

Come back, please come back, my love,
in such absence I've confused autumn
with beauty, and the wind, my love,
the wind cannot tell itself from grass.

A Brief Epistle to Those Who Worked
These Fields and Are Now Long Dead

You would recognize this:
how the zigzag wind snaps each suspended leaf
into gorgeous violence. From the threshold
of wicker chairs we let those tremulous parts
of ourselves shimmer and float, dusk the complexion
of my lost sister's face. Know ten things but tell
only nine, the Taoists like to say. Because they must
our labs push the wet-triangles of their snouts
through a snarl of vetch. Sudden charity, the calculated
strike, if pressed I would argue against the idea
of deciding what we trusted even though it failed us
is altogether wrong. To the north a hawk circles
and uncircles. Feed corn awaits the next thunderburst.
You would apprehend how we're mostly
exhausted, somnambulists without legs.
Hours slump and fall away. Pressed apples
won't preserve a lake yet we drink on the chance
of orchards in the throat. Another leaf, another
scent the faithful can pursue. Across the road
and over the hill come the muffled shouts
of parents, their cleated daughters, the impulse
to balance our constant need for others
with the rapture of aloneness, these cumulus
afternoons when clouds appear as themselves
and not as themselves, as we appear and disappear
to ourselves, until it becomes perfectly impossible
to know the things we say we know, to separate
the flesh from so many alabaster begging bowls
held out to the sun.

Inquiries and Meanderings: Almost a Love Poem

I admit we ought to say something
about the q's in Albuquerque, the bright
sadness of just-painted rooms,
guitar licks and the bones

in our feet, how the cat
has evolved into a self-
cleaning oven, our summer cocktails
so fond of their little umbrellas.

If language must travel in search
of substance then look for what
is sharp on the vine, procrastination
that plot we know best.

Who will volunteer to squeeze
the rusted channel locks, kneel
before the Phillips' dull cross?
That which we could not do

will forever change what we did—
the fatal distances between
Colombian villages, the way she squirts
a cloud of perfume, waits

a moment, then suddenly
walks through. Some argue
that constraint is our only chance,
gutturals and sibilants, how each

climax pokes famously at death.
Shouldn't we shout *apostate!*
when others demand allegiance?
It's painful to watch the k's

in Kilkenny take a burst of jabs
below the belt. Many a good
hanging prevents a bad marriage,
said Shakespeare's twelfth fool.

The organ in the loft is a Sunday
carnival, a red cyclops the van's
maintenance required light. What else?—
besides the hornets that bolt

from their multiplication tables.
A house of waves, a book
of smoke, as usual, my dear,
you are mostly right.

Enough

The hay is in the barn.
The dew is on the baler.

The beer is in the fridge.
The bills are on the table.

How lonely and particular
and how strikingly common.

Eros and Thanatos,
the house that's been built

for each of us, along
with the infinite

details of these hours
which arrive as someone

turns the lock or flicks
the light from the porch.

I can't remember
what comes next,

but I think it ends
with a question mark.

Enough, says the body.
Enough, says the brain.

Let's see if you can find
the rest of the world

from the rest of the farm,
the pasture of your fabulous dream.

Dedications

"Seneca" is for Jim & Pat Hancock.

"Ontario" is for Dane Gordon.

"Saranac" is for Kip & Deb Hale.

"What Happens Without Fanfare" is for Pam & Jack
    Erwin.

"Cycling Through Taylor's Basin" is for Paul Miller.

"Vitamins or Nautilus" is for Stephen Dunn.

"Having Evolved from Stones" is for Lucille Clifton &
    Anthony Piccione.

"August Evening, Bright Hill Farm" is for Bertha Rogers
    & Ernie Fishman.

"Cheesehead" is for Michael Cashin.

"When the Mother of the Bride Is Dying" is for Maria
    Rader & Greg Gale.

"Moonfabulousmoonfib" is for Kurt Brown.

"We Cannot Buy Cliffs Notes" is for Judith E. Gordon &
    Thomas R. Ward.